I0002316

# ZERO TO
# PODCAST

### BY
## HOLLY SHANNON

# DEDICATION

*This is for you. The creator in you. You may not see it yet, but by the end of this book, you will be calling yourself a podcaster.*

# TABLE OF CONTENTS

# INTRODUCTION

When I started my journey, I had no experience. The pandemic decimated my career. I will admit that this was not the first time that life presented me with a teaching moment.

I wasn't alone. The world has had to reinvent, recalibrate and innovate.

I think it's hard to believe, but I stumbled into podcasting completely by accident. I hadn't always dreamed of being 'on-air'. I even had stage fright, no job, imposter syndrome and a myriad of other feelings that could have stopped me in my tracks. It was a leap of faith. What would I lose really? It's not a marketing tool that costs much. I could do it virtually for free.

Well, let's have a heart-to-heart chat about all this.

Finances are not a barrier to entry, and I'll provide you with all the tools for free or close to free.

The stage fright we can work through. I will do my best to share with you the ways to overcome or alleviate some of that. It has worked for me effectively I might add.

Imposter syndrome? Let's unpack that a bit. Your goal here is to share your voice. You do not need to be an expert. You could be, but it is not a prerequisite to podcasting. Remember this, you are finding a community of people that find what you're discussing interesting. It is your job to be curious, not to be an expert. Interview people that bring that to the table. Share their knowledge with them and let it shine through your curiosity. No imposter here!

Jobless? Perhaps building something will give you confidence. It will also give you a way to meet people. This could open doors to connections, business relationships and many other things that you can monetize later.

*Bottom line, you can start from zero.*

*I launched my podcast in 3 weeks. It is entirely possible.*

Everyone moves at their own speed. Everyone has different levels of technical expertise. Some people have the ability to outsource parts of the production of the podcast and some people will do it all. There is no right or wrong way. But I will say this, with no money and no experience, it's 100% possible.

Over time, as I've created content through my podcast, for websites and social media. I wanted to design a book that did not have an excess of words but a concise blueprint to get this done, quickly.

My goal is to get you on public podcast sites like iTunes and Spotify quickly with this step-by-step guide. If you follow my methodology, you will create your podcast.

*In fact, today you are not quite at zero.*

*You have an idea brewing for a podcast, so you are on your way.*

*You can do this, ready to launch? Let's get started!*

# Chapter 1
# Conceptualize your Business Plan

## Who is Your Audience?

Understanding who your show is for is a critical examination of your podcast. You will be asked this question by others. Knowing your audience and the content they'd be interested in listening to are the building blocks to a successful podcast.

Are you talking to your audience solo about your expertise in a certain area?

Are you talking to business executives? Car enthusiasts? Knowing this will allow you to thoughtfully think of who you would like to interview and the relevant topics. Make a list of both. And make a 'reach for the stars' list. You never know who will say yes unless you ask! Having high aspirations is a great way to look at your podcast.

How far can you go within topics, how deep the dive? In what directions can you go for a small series with the idea? It's perfectly ok to roll-out a part one and two with a guest. Or a 5-part series around one idea.

In my humble opinion, nothing kicks doors open like a cold email asking a potential guest to come on your podcast. That, having been said, topics will inspire which guest you invite and possibly vice versa. Pick the top three topics/interviews for your launch. We will discuss why there are three later.

Think about what your audience wants and cares about. If this is your area of expertise or just your general interest, then dive in with that thought process. What is missing in the market? What conversations are not happening? These are ways to see how you'll position your voice.

## Psychographic vs. Demographic?

This is a conversation worth having because podcasting is a unique species. You will never be able to determine the demographics of your audience. Not at the stage podcasting metrics are in 2021. This may change. But until it does, any guest that asks you this question before deciding whether to come on or any advertiser that asks this before buying a spot on your show, will be asking the wrong question. So, what is the question? The answer to this is, "What is the psychographic?" Think more community or tribe here. For example, let's say you have a business podcast that is about company culture. Lindsay is an executive at a Fortune 500 company. She is 40 years old, married and has two children. She lives in New York. Those are demographics. What should you, your guests and advertisers be thinking about? They should be aware of the fact that Lindsay cares about company culture. She wants to work with a company that cares about her growth as a leader in her field. Lindsay may need remote work and time off with her kids. Managing stress are things XYZ company, host and podcast care about and will discuss. She's looking for her community. Does your podcast fit that psychographic? Has she found her tribe of like-minded thinkers that will expand her knowledge and help her grow and learn? The Scribe Method by Tucker Max and Zach Obront discuss this in greater detail from the vantage point of publishing a book. However, I feel creating a podcast carries the same argument. They say, "*understanding the difference is important in modern marketing. The reality is that demographic data used to be all you needed to target and understand audiences because so much of the market fell into predictable patterns based on demographics. Digital media has exploded consumer options and made demographics less predictive of human behavior. Now psychographics work better.*"

## Where Does Your Audience Hang Out?

I ask this question because social media will be an important tool to get the word out. You will be looking for an audience. For example: is your podcast business related? Perhaps your target market lives on LinkedIn and Twitter. This positioning will tap into the biggest audience for you. If your podcast is about clothing design, your target market would possibly live on Instagram and Pinterest.

Think about why the show benefits listeners. Ensure that what you bring to the table to talk about will be compelling, informative and thought provoking. Or it may be light, a guilty diversion and funny. Benefiting listeners can mean many things.

By thinking about the target market now, you may identify advertisers and sponsors that you can reach out to later when you monetize your podcast. Downloads = monetization. No one will be interested until you have a substantial audience. We'll talk about monetization later.

## What is your Podcast Name and Description?

It is your elevator speech and it's essential. The description will be your intro and what potential subscribers see when they search for your podcast or your genre. So, I may use description and intro somewhat interchangeably.

## Does Anyone Else Have This Podcast?

It's good to think about how your audience will find your podcast when they Google search you. This search could happen in Google or directly in the places they listen from, i.e., iTunes and Spotify.

Don't be esoteric, be purposeful. Search words you would use if you wanted to know about a subject, like business management, financial markets, car repair. Know that this exercise will help you confirm your name, description and other podcasts like you. Don't be surprised if the name you wanted has been taken or really close to what you wanted. The good news is that listeners may subscribe to you and your competition to find the one they like better, so that could be advantageous. However, if the titles are too close for comfort, you run the risk of the other podcast being chosen. Everyone is busy and perhaps they want their subscriptions curated so they don't have an overload on one topic.

Nevertheless, there is room for everyone. Podcasting is on the rise. There is a place for your voice. Your listeners are waiting for you, your ideas and your voice.

## Find me with Keywords...

When people search for a new podcast, they enter keywords to get them there. As mentioned, car repair, financial markets, etc. You'll use this later when you build each episode into the Podcast Host. So, start making a list. Think about any Google search you've ever done on a specific topic. The goal is to rank for these words. It's the world of SEO (Search Engine Optimization). You will likely not compete with the big-name podcasts here because they have budgets to hire people specifically for this. But do your best and build this list into every episode.

I like to keep a pad next to me when I'm editing for two reasons:

1) Keywords come up during the interview that you can capture for the episode and for the future. For example, maybe it is corporate meetings you are discussing, and your guest says, 'company retreat' or 'conferences'. These can all be added. Also, add your name and the guest to the keywords. Spell them correctly and incorrectly. Separate first and last name, and add them as one word, forwards and backwards.

2) While editing you can listen for the tidbit that you'd like to feature before the intro to the podcast if you are interested. Again, this is not a must, just a matter of preference. You may also catch a 30-60 second piece of audio that you could repurpose later in an Audiogram. I'll touch on this later, and the content you create can be used again and again. So, if something an interviewee said truly resonates with you or your audience, find various ways to present it.

# Chapter 2
# Starting with your Vision

It's the Combination of the Name and Podcast Art that bring your Inspiration to Life.

## Determine the name and concept behind it:

Example Name: Tech Builders

Example Concept: conversations with start-up founders and established company heads about how they got started in technology.

Check iTunes, Spotify and Google search the name to see if it already exists.

Check if there are URL's already associated with it too. In the event you want to start a website with your podcast one day, it's good to know if your podcast name will direct the search to someone else's business (URL) through your marketing efforts.

Create podcast art. I use Canva. Their service is free. As you expand your podcast and want other marketing tools, they have it all, at a low fee. These added fees can expand availability of font choices and features you may want for branding yourself and your podcast.

Determine the aesthetic: Will you have just words, a logo, your picture, something animated or a sketch? There is no right or wrong way here. I've researched and have found that all styles are used fairly equally. There will always be trends, of course, but what appeals to you? Do you like graphics of letters? Prefer to show your picture? Think about this. Create a couple of formats before you decide. After one simple check in "New and Noteworthy" on iTunes, you'll see there is no one way. There is a balance of just name and host, some with pictures, and some without. So, choose what resonates with you.

Some examples below that are just words, with images, etc.

Don't dismiss this step. It is your brand look, and it is what catches attention. You'll use it for a long time. Enjoy this process and test it out if you have a couple of mock-ups. Share it with your most artistic friend.

Opening iTunes and looking up Podcasts, you can pull up your Canva art and size it in Preview to match the rough size as seen on your laptop or phone. This will help to visualize if you love it and, more importantly, can read it. What you see on the screen is vastly smaller than when you created the artwork, so you want to be sure all is legible - name, host, etc.

The format is square. If Canva or the app you use does not have 'podcast art' as a choice, choose a custom setup for the required square format. The pixel size is 3000 x 3000 max. @72dpi and will display as 125 x 125 pixels. It is great to look on your mobile device on iTunes and Spotify to get a sense of the actual size visually. This step is critical, as words, titles, subtitles and logos can easily get lost if you shrink it to fit your phone. I recommend this exercise. I used screenshots and held it up to my laptop and put it side-by-side with iTunes to see how it stood out or didn't!

Create a folder on your desktop and name it 'Podcast Art'. Put all the downloaded finished files here. I suggest you not only put the square formatted podcast art in this folder but create things like Facebook and LinkedIn banners. You will want podcast art sized specifically for the social media site(s) you will use. Once you have the finished podcast art, the other formats are quick. They are great to have for updating your profiles to reflect your new business venture or passion project. Always download in .png or .jpg because they are universally accepted.

# Chapter 3
# The Nuts & Bolts

## What Costs are Involved for Equipment and Podcast Host?

These days you can record on your phone. So, don't let the lack of funds derail you from creating. However, having a decent microphone and headset can ensure better quality and a consistent sound. Use what you have, improve later.

When you are ready, I use the <u>Samson Q2U microphone USB/XLR</u> and headset. It is the 'starter option'. It works well, I'll likely not upgrade from here. Amazon had a special kit price for the mic, headset, tripod and applicable wires for about $70. Many people use the <u>AT200 USB/XLR</u> mic. It was out of stock and around $80 for microphone alone so I went budget-friendly and got the whole set. Samson has also been around a long time, so I was confident the sound quality would be great. I have no affiliation with them, by the way.

Feel free to Google search and see what others say, but I'll tell you that everything I saw generally came down to those two products. They spoke of super high-end mics that are not worth the spend if you are just starting out. Remember, there will always be something newer and cooler on the market. Choose the path of 'good' if it means you'll get this done.

## Who will Host your Podcast?

There are many Podcast Hosts that are free or have an introductory window at least until you get your feet wet. I use Simplecast. It's worth researching them to see what suits your general path. For example: Podbean offers private integration in case you want to use it as a tool within your company and do not intend to broadcast to the world through iTunes, etc. Podbean is also free. Some offer an assist in monetization. All offer a website landing page that will showcase your podcast art, description and list the podcast recordings in episode order. Nevertheless, they are all similar enough that you will likely be happy with your choice. It's merely the nuances that might be important to you if your goal is different from the general podcast. They all broadcast your RSS feed across the platforms most are interested in i.e., iTunes, Spotify, PocketCasts, iHeart Radio, etc.

I might add that the necessity for a separate website is not necessary as Simplecast and some of the Podcast Hosts mentioned do that for you. If you want to further brand yourself and the show, you can explore that later.

As for Simplecast, which I have no affiliation with, it's about $15 a month. You can upgrade later if you grow.

I'm not into choices that limit by upload hours. Part of your branding might include a time frame. For example, you may want to keep it at 20 minutes for the classic commute time. I have found that good conversation and exceptional content shouldn't be capped. In fact, forcing the 20 minutes is not desirable for me. Guests sometimes take 5 or more minutes to warm up before the conversation flows more naturally.

## What Should I Record On?

I prefer <u>Zencastr</u> to record. At the moment, they are offering a "hobbyist" account that is free. Generally, the charge is $20 a month, but even if you must pay, I believe it is worth it.

<u>Zoom</u>, if you've used it and experienced lag time then you'll know that it can happen while recording your podcast. I had too many incidences of voices recording on top of each other and sections of lag that were irreparable. You don't want to edit out good content because of sound or recording issues. Rerecording those sections could work but is not ideal. Unfortunately, you do not learn this until the editing phase and possibly find yourself halfway in and have to scrap it all.

There are ways to mitigate this with Zoom or other recording companies. You can use the single track that features the guests and hosts. This will work for the occasional problem, but you are unable to edit out cars, dogs, notifications, etc. But, yes, it's a good occasional solution. Nevertheless, sometimes you are left with editing disasters and time wasted.

Why Zencastr? Because it records locally on each computer. So, the finished downloads are much cleaner. In fact, I've been able to forego using a sound software to clean up the finished MP3. In the past I recorded in Zoom, edited in GarageBand and then ran it through Auphonics to clean it up before uploading to the Podcast Host. I can skip that step now.

You need to remind your guest at the close of your interview to keep their browser open until the computer downloads the podcast, but that is nearly instantaneous once you click the record button off.

When you create your account, you go to the Dashboard, name the interview, copy the link and email your guests, done!

# Chapter 4
# Pre-Production Hygiene

## Where Intro and Description Meet...

Every podcast needs an introduction. Record yourself or ask a friend with a good voice. There are also companies that provide voice for hire. In the end, you will be the voice of the podcast, so get comfortable. You should try different intros, tones, with or without music, etc.

Ideally you want to clearly state what the podcast is about in about 2 to 3 sentences. I would suggest not much more for two reasons:

1) In time, when you monetize, you may have an ad or sponsor at the top of the podcast that will run before you begin your interview.
2) You may also want to pre-record an intro for each guest. You can easily be 2-3 minutes into the start before the interview actually begins.

You want to keep your listener's attention. Do keep the podcast description and the intro unique to each guest, along with being concise!

# What Should I Consider Before Recording?

Leading up to recording consider doing the following if you like structure over spontaneity:

1) Have an exploratory call with your guest.
2) On this call, tap into the idea for the show with them. Remember, you are leaning in on their expertise to create a good exchange. This is your opportunity to see if there is, in fact, a story to tell.
3) After the call, put together the questions or outline that best reflects the direction and structure of the interview to come.
4) Ask for their bio (short version, or ask permission to take it from their LinkedIn profile or their website if they have either)
5) Secure the interview date on this call. It will save you time emailing back-and-forth to find a mutual time.
6) Calendly also offers a free scheduling service if you want to incorporate that. Parking a specific day(s) for exploratory calls and actual interviews is great hygiene for structure if you crave that!

Flow in the conversation is always great. Pauses that linger may feel uncomfortable for both parties. So, having a few questions ready that allow the conversation to have a beginning, middle and end is important.

Remember, they are likely the expert. Have questions ready and be comfortable letting it go off script. Sometimes that is where the magic is. One tip I received from another podcaster is if you find an unpleasant pause or you need a way to close the podcast, ask your guest this question, "what haven't I asked you that you'd like to share with the listeners?"

## Should we address nerves?

Hosting a solo podcast, interviewing guests or co-hosting all present the person behind the microphone occasionally with nerves. Public speaking takes time to get right. And yes, I'm sure you expect me to say that everyone is nervous, or it goes away. What I will say, however, is that everyone is different. I am always nervous before recording with a guest, always. But I will say this, it is a muscle. It gets stronger. It gets easier with repetition and a consistent structure. Creating a format in the podcast and communicating with your guest, brings consistency. This helps eliminate some fear that could derail your confidence. You will feel that the framework is solid. You have given your guests everything they need for a successful podcast and you prepared with the exploratory call and questions.

You got this! There is only one voice on this topic right now, it's yours. Use it, enjoy, play, create, and allow yourself to laugh occasionally. There will be flubs and I promise that you are not alone in that. You are not alone in your fears, but it will get better with time, structure and repeated use of your new muscle. Go make your podcast! Episode 10 will be exponentially better than the first 5. Episode 50 will be light years away from episode 10.

*Grow, be patient with yourself, think of your microphone as a hand weight. The more you lift it, the stronger you get.*

## Why Should I Email?

That email will be very professional and helpful for the guest if it encompasses more than the questions. It allows you to be sure everyone is on the same page. There are a few other details to include that I think are critical:

1) Email the confirmation of the recording to include the date and time, including time zone.
2) Email the guest those questions/outline you determined in the exploratory call. This is a good opportunity for them to revise anything and be prepared for the interview.
3) Include the Zencastr link or whatever recording software you choose.
4) Title of the podcast episode (this can still be determined or modified post interview if you feel that the title will be more obvious to you then).
5) Guest intro: a brief bio of the guest and the subject to be discussed. Note: This can be pre-recorded, or

you can present that as the lead-in to saying hello and welcome your guest on-air.

6) Request a headshot, any links to their social media or website to be included in the show notes. (you'll add those when you upload the episode to the Podcast Host), more on that later.

7) Should you include a podcast release form or not? This is up to you based on its end use. If you are a large company and want to protect the audio for your use in content for websites and social media, or in any capacity, you'll want this.

8) There are Podcast Guest Release Forms out there. Some searching on your part will probably unearth a template.

9) Below is an example of the language I use and would likely suffice. I'm not a lawyer. If it matters enough to you, seek one.

*Hi (guest name here),*

*We are looking forward to having you on the podcast! We are scheduled for August 10, 2020 on Zencastr at 11:00 am EST. (insert link here).*

*It will be an audio recording with no video on.*

*Intro:*

*(Insert guest bio and lead in for interview here)*

*Questions: (create and add here from exploratory call)*

*1.*

*2.*

*3.*

*Once the interview is recorded, it becomes the property of (insert podcast name here) and may be used in various mediums for promotional or developmental purposes. Both you and your business or organization will always be properly credited.*

*Once the interview has been recorded and deemed appropriate to become a part of the podcast series, you will be notified of the date it will be released. It is at this point that you are free to publicize the interview by any means you see fit.*

*By scheduling an interview, you are indicating that you agree with these stipulations.*

*Please send me the URL links you'd like included in the show notes and a picture to use on our website and on social media.*

# Here are a Few Tidbits...

Be consistent, it's part of what your listeners will look forward to. Choose the day your episode will air and schedule it on the Podcast Host to drop that day.

There is no one size fits all formula. It could be once a week, twice a month or once a month. Whatever you want.

Think about the length. As I mentioned, some people subscribe to the 20-minute commute theory. Others feel the content is too good to limit and will share an hour's worth of conversation.

Consistency means choosing a couple of days specifically for exploratory calls and emails. It is also critical for structure to be consistent and to allot specific days for recording and days for editing. This may or may not bother you. But if you are co-hosting or pulling guests from all over the world, it may help streamline your work.

I think it's important to send a thank you to each guest the day before the podcast drops to let them know all the relevant links to share with their Following. Cross-pollinate Followers! Below is a sample letter you could use:

*Hi (insert name here),*

*Let me thank you for spending the time and talking about your leadership style during this time. I truly believe our listeners will benefit from your expertise and authentic voice.*

*We are in the final stretch of launching your podcast, which drops tomorrow. We are so thrilled with the outcome. Please feel free to share the links below with friends and colleagues as we'd love to spread the word.*

*You'll see my posts on LinkedIn, Instagram, Facebook and Twitter.*

*Follow me there so we can continue the conversation.*

*(insert your tags here and consider hyperlinking them so it looks clean)*

*iTunes: https://apple.co/2Ky0NGk*

*Google Play: https://bit.ly/2KLmAKN*

*Spotify: https://spoti.fi/3ePWfsG*

*Also on PocketCasts, Stitcher, iHeart radio....if you want these links, please advise.*

*Also, we will continue the conversation on LinkedIn. We look forward to engaging our listeners with you there!*

## Setting up Recording Software:

I use GarageBand. It is free with Apple devices. Audacity is another free one. Some prefer ProTools. There may be others, Google to find the one that works best with your computer software.

1) Be sure your computer has uploaded the latest software.
2) Set-up microphone as an input device.
3) Do several tests to ensure the settings are to your liking.

## Pointers for when you record:

1) Hook up your equipment and connect headset to the microphone and the microphone to your computer with the USB cable provided. The equipment you bought will have the directions in greater detail and hopefully you already installed and tested it by the time you have reached this point in this book.
2) Do not move the microphone. Use a stand or tripod.
3) Be consistent in your distance from the microphone.
4) Use a windscreen, if possible, to reduce popping which occurs often with certain words.
5) Minimize distractions by silencing your phone. Turn off notifications on your phone and computer and remind your guests to do the same.

6) Choose a location that is small and has the least amount of distractions and sounds. A closet works well, by the way.

7) You will meet your guest the day of recording on Zencastr or Zoom where you created the link.

8) When you hit the record button, confirm that your guest sees the blinking red light.

9) It is very important not to shut off or restart your recording during the interview. The files obtained through Zencastr or Zoom will be difficult to edit.

10) Rather than shutting off, just pause with your guest and ask to re-record the question. Interruptions of kids, dogs, emergency vehicles, notifications, etc. will happen. Keep rolling for continuity if you can and if not, pause and repeat the question.

11) It will be easier to edit if you pause vs. turning the recording off and back on. Just keep going!

## Shall we Skim the Basics for Templates in GarageBand?

This is not a complete manual for all the recording software. YouTube and your software choice will have tutorials. This is my distillation in GarageBand and will be a good framework for what you will do. For some, it may be enough. As I mentioned in the beginning, some of us will be more technically proficient than others. This is not to scare you away, but to encourage you to learn using all the tutorials at your disposal. There are a lot of great people out there walking you slowly and meticulously through the steps needed.

As an aside, you can outsource all pre and postproduction. Many do!

# CHAPTER 5
# PRODUCTION

## Can we Walk Through Creating a GarageBand Template?

Choose a Track Type:

Audio/Microphone

Input 1

Connect to Microphone

Create

Modify settings:

Drop down menu to (check mark) Time

Toggle off metronome and Count-in 1234

Choose:

Track Master Compare

Input 1 (Microphone, mine is Samson)

Minimize the library icon or it will drive you crazy like it did me.

File: Save As

Save as Template to Desktop, you can use this again and again.

You can update this template even further by pre-recording your intro with music and do a "Save As" for that one.

If the Podcast is only you are recording solo, you can record in GarageBand or directly on your own computer's software. This method could be used if there are two people in the same room for every recording. For example: if you and a friend are recording your conversations.

In this case, recording will be streamlined. You will not need Zencastr or Zoom.

However, if you have a guest or co-host, you'll set-up multitrack recording steps:

1) Name the first track by double clicking and placing your name on Track One.

2) Next you will click 'add a track', followed by, 'input 2' (your microphone), finishing by renaming the new track with the guest or co-host name.
3) Minimize the library if this bothers you.
4) Go to the Track toolbar and pull-down to configure the track header.
5) Click Record.
6) Select Record buttons on each individual track.
7) When flashing, the individual tracks will record simultaneously when the Master Record button is clicked in the Track Header.
8) You can add more people too.
9) Record in GarageBand, and backup a recording in Quicktime if you are at all concerned!

## Some Basic Editing Techniques:

There will be three techniques that will allow you to do that basic editing.

1) Trim,
2) Split at PlayHead
3) Automation Tool

Because they are all slightly different, I recommend YouTube tutorials. They will allow you to explore and refine these techniques by allowing you to pause and practice.

There is plenty of free music on GarageBand, so choose an intro and outro that you like. In the spirit of producing for free or really close, use that to start. You can always upgrade later if it's important to you.

## Episode Structure:

Generally, everyone starts their podcast in one of two ways:

1)   A tidbit of the interview to bait the listener to listen
2)   Starting with the music overlaying the podcast intro

You can use 1 and follow with 2, or just start with 2.

For the sake of continuing with this section, let's assume you are now at step 2. Your music will be at a level low enough to hear the intro but high enough to make it sound robust and exciting. Using your Automation Tool here in the techniques above, you can choose that level and you can have the music ascend at the beginning and descend toward the end of this intro.

If you build this into your template, it'll be there every episode and you will only need to add the newest interview each time.

Your next step is the introduction that is specific to your interviewee. If you recall, you will work with that guest to build their bio and to engage your listeners with their experience and sense of the interview to come. (This was the purpose behind the exploratory call).

The step to follow the interview is the music again, known as the outro.

You can place narration here if you like. Perhaps you want to enlighten your listeners about the next podcast, for example, "Next week, listen in as we talk with (insert name here)"

While it is premature, when you get to the point of monetizing your podcast, you will try to sell advertisements and sponsorships to cover your costs. Ultimately, you will design a cost structure to reflect the best places to hear those ads. These are placed at the beginning, mid-roll and end and are priced highest to lowest, respectively.

## How to Export in GarageBand:

Upload the file as MP3. You can do a WAV file, but I find it most compatible with the Podcast Hosts.

1) Go to menu bar
2) Click on Share: pull down to Export song to disk
3) Save As (create podcast name here) and where you want it saved
4) Choose MP3: choose bit-rate or quality at 128
5) Hit export

You'll watch the playhead scrub the entire episode, export it to an MP3 file, normalize the audio and boom! You have your finished product!

- Store under "documents" in your Finder
- You now have a finished file to upload to the Host.
- You can run this through Auphonics to refine the sound, if you choose. It is free based on how many hours you use.
- If you choose to do this step, Open Finder and under Documents you should have the MP3 at your disposal.

In iTunes on your computer, you will find your podcast as the MP3 you created.

I would suggest creating a playlist here with the podcast name and dragging the file into it so they are all together. Click on the 3 vertical dots at the right-hand side and add to the Playlist.

You can embed ID tags here as well and this is Podcast Host friendly:

Go into the MP3 and Click on the 3 vertical dots at the right-hand side and pull down to Get Info:

Under Details, fill-in all or which ones you want.

It is designed for Song Info not for podcast info, so some things won't apply:

- Title
- Artist name
- Album name
- Album artist

- Composer
- Publishing year
- Genre of podcast
- Comments (intro description about the guest)

As I mentioned earlier on, Zencastr records locally on each person's computer. I find the sound quality very good. I don't personally find it necessary to take the MP3 file created in Garageband and upload it to Auphonics. This is a software to optimize your audio algorithms by analyzing and tweaking them. They have 2 hours you can sign up for that are free or pay for more. I believe this is better for pro-level podcasting.

## An important side trick:

Keep a pad next to you when you are listening to your recording. Mark down any words that you think someone would search for or any names of companies or people that your guest used. It will make it easier later when you upload your episode on the Podcast Host. You'll have this list of words to enter. It can be a bit of an annoying task, but I think the more tag/keywords you add, the better for optimizing searches. I realize this is repetitive, but a good reminder.

## Another tip:

Mark off any 30-60 second bit of the show that stands out to you. You'll need to remember the 'second point' that it begins and ends in the final cut of your podcast. For example, you like a piece of the conversation that starts at 12:37 and ends at 13:12 seconds. You can use this later in a couple of ways:

- You can add this to the very beginning of your podcast to give listeners a taste of your show, enticing them at the start so they are excited to dig in.
- You can also use this piece later to Recast and create an Audiogram. (I'll discuss this later in the book but highlight this part if it interests you. This is not something you must do, it's just another way to reuse your content. It is also a visual representation of the podcast, so it makes for a dynamic post.)

## If this next section scares you, leave it off:

Nevertheless, should you decide to do this step, here's a short Auphonic's tutorial:

Go to New Production

Choose file

Skip intro and outro

Skip metadata, extended metadata and chapter marks

Click on Output Files

- Format MP3: 128kbps
- Bitrate: optimal
- Mono: check this and at 19 LUFS
- Sample Rate 44.1 KHz
- Bit Depth: 32-bit float or 24-bit
- MP3 type: constant bit rate (CBR)

(these are the optimal settings for Simplecast, it's probable that Auphonics won't ask for all of these)

Skip Speech Recognition and Publishing

Click on Audio Algorithms

Check the following:

- Adaptive Leveler (will even out all tracks)
- Filtering (for filtering out background noise)
- Loudness Normalization (set volume at right level)
- Loudness Target (19 LUFS for monofiles, stereo mixes aren't as loud as mono)

Don't check off Noise and Hum. Try to create your very best recording environment. If you must click it, choose Auto for Reduction Amount.

Start Production

After processing it will show you the statistics. You can click input on the bottom to see the difference between what you put in and what Auphonic put out.

In the menu bar, click download. It will be the file that you can use for the Podcast Host, like Simplecast.

## After Download:

Go to Preset in the top menu bar and you can save this setup for every podcast. This will be your Auphonics Template and each time you return with a new episode you will choose Preset from the drop-down menu to Podcast Audio.

Auphonics is not great with fade-outs. The software can chop them up and it can be a bit jarring. If you are perfecting that, you may be disappointed in their results.

This service is free for 2 hours a month.

Keep your files neat and accessible:

- Desktop files make your life easier.
- Create a master folder with the Podcast Name.
- Create a subfolder called Recordings.
  - You will create a folder in here with each new episode.
  - Adding the Zencastr files along with the final episode is a good idea.

There are freelance websites that can do a lot of the work you do not want to do. In my humble opinion, I think it is wise to do everything in the beginning. Here's the motivational speech in 3 points:

1) *Ownership feels good.*
2) *Learning can be scary, but it makes you stronger.*
3) *If you don't know what you need, it is harder to ask for it and to ensure you get what you want.*

Upwork, TaskRabbit, and LinkedIn...reach out for help when you are ready.

As mentioned, most software provides tutorials, YouTube, Skillshare and more.

# Chapter 6
# Uploading to Podcast Host

I have mentioned Simplecast from the beginning. There are others. Some let you start for free; some have a small monthly fee; some will help you monetize your show. Most of them will create a landing page type of website. This is professional looking and takes the effort out of creating a website as well. You can use the unique link created by this Podcast Host for all of your social media posts or specifically use your link to iTunes, Spotify, etc.

## Let's Get Started!

A $15 monthly fee will get you started with most of them. This will give you 2 member seats which is great because if you decide to bring in a production team or someone well-versed in studying the metrics, you have a way to let them assist in the process without full control.

As I mentioned, you get that landing page with a slightly customizable website that has its own domain. The caveat here is the slight part. You will have your podcast art and episodes. You will not be able to do much more except add color to the background. You will not be able to build a blog. However, if you decide to have your episodes transcribed, this will improve your SEO (Search Engine Optimization). This ability to add transcription is part of the available features of your Podcast Hosted website. You can also increase this metric by adding tag words into your episodes. As I break down the process of using the Podcast Host, I'll refer back to that.

Each Podcast Host will have a variety of other features. For example, high download capability, secure RSS feed, email support and multiple shows. You need to compare the different platforms. That all being said, do not get too caught up in this part. They are all pretty comparable in price and service.

Once you create your new account, congratulations by the way, you are nearly there. Below are the steps in Simplecast and as mentioned, most of them will have similar requested components.

1) Create a new show.
2) Enter Title.
3) Enter description (this is important), spend the time necessary. If you recall, it's your elevator speech. It is what your potential listeners will see when they are browsing podcasts to follow. A short paragraph with 2-5 sentences is all you need. The shorter the better. Think of keywords that a consumer of podcasts

would search for. We addressed this earlier in this book. (see chapter one).

4) Upload your artwork. This is the podcast art you created in Canva.

5) Enter your format, this will most likely be 'episodic', showing your newest episodes first.

6) Enter the time zone.

7) Enter the language.

8) Enter if there will be explicit content. If your show is anything close to Joe Rogan, then check that box. Your listeners will decide if they are ok with it. Alternatively, as you upload episodes, you can select per episode if it only applies to certain or occasional ones.

9) Categorize, this will be important. You'll have more than one to choose from. The platforms that carry your show will want to park you in the appropriate sections to make it easier for their own categorization. For example, Business, Pop-culture, etc.

10) Tags are so important! Back to Chapter one and keywords. Add as many as they will allow to help listeners find you.

11) Owner Details: add yourself as the author and anyone else credited with the content if you are co-hosting or co-producing.

12) Add yourself as Show Owner and it will request your email as well.

13) Copyright: enter the podcast name here.

Once the core is built, this will be your de facto template, and all will apply to each new episode you upload. Now let's upload!

1) Create New Episode
2) Add the Title of the episode, it will create a URL address for it automatically. If there are keywords in your title, along with the guest name, this is a searchable URL also.
3) Input the MP3 file created. Some are drag & drop, some upload from your computer and you can access your MP3 file here.
4) Add Show Notes: profile addresses of hosts, guests, relevant websites discussed in the episode, links to books or anything you'd like to add here.
5) Add Tags.
6) You can add cover art here if you want each episode to look different. Or you can keep it as the cover art you entered at the beginning. This will default and you won't be required to re-add it each time you upload a new episode.
7) Add the episode description. I would keep this to about 3 sentences if possible. Include the guest name, title, company and storyline. Remember to use keywords for those robust SEOs and make it interesting sounding to catch the potential listener. Each episode is unique; tell them why it is here. The bonus is this will likely already be available to you. Why is that? Because it was your intro to your listeners when you went into the interview to

introduce and greet your guest. So at least it minimizes the extra work.

8) Add your transcript. It's a good practice for two compelling reasons:
    a) If you eventually have a website, the transcription will be a great SEO mechanism.
    b) It will also allow you to repurpose content in written form for posting.

Free services like Otter, offer a transcript that is pretty good, but not great. It will suffice for starting out. If just starting out, choose free services. You can read through it and manually adjust if it didn't translate perfectly. Paid services like Rev are a better quality but can cost you a lot of money. There are also people that do this for a living, so check out groups like TaskRabbit, Fiverr and Upwork.

1) The next step is scheduling the episode. As you may recall from a previous chapter, the day you regularly drop an episode will be important for consistency. Your listeners will look forward to each week on Tuesday if you establish that schedule.

2) Guess what? You did it! Your episode now has a unique RSS (Really Simple Syndication) that will be sent to platforms of your choice.

## So which platforms?

I suggest you send this RSS (Really Simple Syndication) link to as many as you like. You can send them to all the platforms, i.e., iTunes, Spotify, PocketCasts, Google Play, iHeartRadio, Audible etc.

Click on each distribution platform and attach the RSS feed to each one. Not all platforms are available to all. Android phones do not have Apple Podcasts. Your friends may have Spotify and use that exclusively with their iPhone or Samsung or laptop. Subscribe to any and all!

Each one will likely have you register on their site and will walk you through some easy steps.

What is most important here is that you make sure that each one you plan to advertise/use has received your request and returned an email with their permission and clearance. They will send you an email congratulating you on inclusion. Some take longer than others! I received iTunes sooner than expected, but iHeart Radio took very long. They will all provide you with your unique link. Basically, you can expect these platforms to respond in 1-4 weeks. The caveat here is that you do not want to jump on social media announcing you are 'live' until you are confirmed by each platform. You can do this once you have one or two and then announce the others as they confirm to you in email.

Recently Amazon added podcasts to Audible. Be sure to add to this one. It may not be available through the Podcast Host site, but you can access this directly through Amazon.

## How Do I Know How I'm Doing? Metrics Please?

Analytics are posted on the Podcast Host, so you can get a look geographically, time of day, etc. where the activity is best. You can alter your posts and Audiogram addition to play into that timing.

Each Host will offer a different version of basic metrics for the basic/starter price. A deeper dive into the analytics is always offered when you pay for a more robust service.

Google Analytics will give you a bigger picture. This is another outlet for the results of your podcast.

# CHAPTER 7
# LAUNCH THAT PODCAST

Industry wide recommendation: Launch three complete episodes and have one in the making. Remember I said three in Chapter One? Here we go! You are almost there podcaster!

Prepare the content/blog posts for each one to be ready for social media and email blast.

Be sure that your episodes have been uploaded to the Podcast Host and are ready for your listeners to subscribe via iTunes, Spotify, etc. Remember, you should receive an email from each of them confirming approval and acceptance.

You can apply to all different ones; I suggest you apply to all of them that the Podcast Host partners with. It is not as time consuming as you think. Everyone has different mobile phones, computers and subscriptions, so you don't want to leave anyone out.

# Should I Include Friends and Family?

Absolutely! Email them your launch date, ask them to subscribe, rate, review and share.

Post on Facebook, Instagram, Twitter, LinkedIn, whatever social media you will use.

Consider creating a page in these specific to your podcast if you want. However, it is not necessary.

Share your podcast art and your first guests to spread interest. Let your guests know of launch day so they can share as well.

iTunes allows you to rate your podcast show (not individual episodes). When your friends upload the podcast, they will see the star rating at the end of the episode description. Writing a review requires them to scroll further down. iTunes makes this a bit discreet. You will see in purple, it will say 'Write a Review'. Click on this and have your friends write something nice.

Ultimately this exercise will help your rankings with the platforms and hopefully move you up to actually being recommended by them! 'New & Noteworthy' is the highest ranking they can give you.

# It is Launch Day!

This is getting very exciting! Publish the 3 blogs you wrote on social media, show-off that beautiful podcast art.

Instagram lets you put a link to the podcast in your profile, but not on the actual post. Let your followers know that when you add your post.

Below is an example in Instagram. This is the same podcast, but a different voice. As I mentioned, your audience might follow you on a couple of platforms. You want your voice to be unique to each and not repetitive content. The guest and the company were tagged so they received the post and could share it.

*"What if we treated employees like Olympic Athletes? No, really!*

*Elena Shannon the Founder of Agile Health Sciences, who just happened to coach in the Rio Olympics is on*

*Culture Factor 2.0*

*#health #podcast #burnout #companyculture #employees #employers"*

Facebook lets you put it directly in the post.

LinkedIn lets you add the link to the podcast in the comments, so you can state that in your post to click there. The algorithms do not like it within the post. You can also add it as a website on your profile there. LinkedIn is very much about algorithms. It actually doesn't like links in the body of the post. It prefers pictures and the link in the comments. If you use that, let your followers know the link is in the comments.

Here's an example of a LinkedIn post below. I also included the podcast art with this. Notice the use of bullet points which can be effective and give order to your ideas. You don't always have to do that. In fact, a line in between can suffice. I also incorporated hashtags within the post but you can put them at the end if it looks too busy when you actually read it. Three to five hashtags are best here. Again, this is LinkedIn algorithm friendly. And LinkedIn also likes emojis.

1) *Elena Shannon the Founder of Agile Health Science is on Culture Factor 2.0.* 👀

2) *What if you treated #employees like Olympic athletes?* 🏃🏃🏃🏃🏃 *Especially if you're scaling or going for a Series round.*

3) *BTW, Elena just so happened to be a Coach in the Rio Olympics.* 🏆🏆🏆🏆🏆🏆🏆

4) *Subscribe and write something down here* 🖊 *bc Elena has the answer to your #health and #burnout questions. Yes, link is in the comments below.*

Twitter lets you put it directly on the tweet and your profile.

*Elena Shannon the Founder of @agilehealth, what if we treated employees like Olympic Athletes? Not posting a picture of me sweating and lifting weights like Serena Williams.*

*(insert link to podcast here)*

*#MentalHealthAwareness #health #podcast #burnout #companyculture #employees #employers #HRTech*

## Side note:

If your link is long because your title is long, you can take the Simplecast link and copy it into Bit.ly to shorten it. This is valuable if you are posting on Twitter which limits total characters. In the above example I left the long title because I had the character length available and there were key words in there.

## Another side note:

You can add "alt" text to pictures you post. This makes the content more searchable!

## Social Media, Personal or Podcast:

You can create pages in Facebook, LinkedIn, Twitter, or Instagram that are specific to your podcast identity. To start, I suggest you keep it personal and on your own pages.

If you are co-hosting, perhaps you'll reconsider that idea. This is fine, but then I would suggest posting on both every time you launch an episode and/or audiogram. I believe the 'personal branding' piece is important. Listeners are tuning into you. It brings warmth and authenticity to the beginning of the show.

Optimize platforms by researching the trending keywords on them so you can be a part of the conversation. Twitter and the like have trending #'s. I tend to play with the use of hashtags for the same podcasts. I use different ones depending on the platform. For LinkedIn I might push hashtags that are more business relevant or seem to be trending on other people's posts. Instagram might be more personally relevant.

Don't forget, whether it is the podcast page or your personal page, put the link to the show in your actual profile so your podcast can always be found.

Varying content from platform to platform is advisable if you have followers that spend time on different social media platforms. Keeping them engaged and sharing your work is important. They could become bored if your postings are duplicated throughout. Perhaps an audiogram, a short video, a picture of a guest, etc.

## Celebrating your Launch?

Absolutely, if you have anyone you follow on social media that has a large following, reach out! You never know who will say yes, until you ask. And that is the same for podcast guests.

# Chapter 8
# Audiograms & Sound Bites

Headliner and Wavve are two sites you can create audiograms with. I think it's a great added piece of content.

I like to post one towards the end of the week that an episode launched. This is where you can recycle the podcast art or use the picture of the guest.

Remember that sound bite you wrote down? Here is where you use it.

1) Using Headliner, you will be able to upload the episode by typing in the name of the podcast. Then you can choose which episode exactly.
2) Drag the cursor to the spot you want to clip. Play it to be sure you don't cut-off important words. You will be able to add seconds at the front and back of it to capture the precise piece of audio.
3) Add podcast art or the guest photo.
4) Add text to include the podcast name and guest name.
5) You can add unique features like a track that shows the voice modulation, color of text or it can even slide the text from one side to the other for a visual feature.

6) When it looks right, play it to be sure and then export the file.
7) You'll find it in your Downloads Folder.
8) Now you can share this across your social media platforms!

# CHAPTER 9
## CONTRACTS

## Should I Have a Podcast Pre-Nup?

Word to the wise, if you are co-hosting or co-producing, always put together a contract. While you may be the best of friends, you'll be surprised at the situations that come up that you could disagree on and so you'll want something more than a handshake and a promise of 50/50 representation. You might disagree about a guest, advertising representation, majority voice, who pays for what, who does the most work, etc. Button this up before to divert problems in the future.

Be clear in the language regarding what share you will each have. Things like majority voice, monetization, use of the podcast, advertising on social media, choice of guest, use of the podcast for other things like books, conferences, etc. are critical conversations. When you see the monetization possibilities below, you'll understand how you can grow your podcast later. Money changes behavior be prepared with your Podcast PreNup! You heard it here!

## And a Guest Contract too?

We spoke about the language in your email to confirm the guest is ok with you using their likeness and name. There are Podcast Release Forms out there that you can print from the internet and serve to each guest as written permission if you want the added layer of protection.

## Other Ways I Should Protect my Passion Project?

Register it. The Writer's Guild has a registration for you. It's an added layer of protection in a co-created relationship. There is an east coast and west coast outpost. I found the east coast version easy.

# CHAPTER 10
## PROMOTION

As your podcast progresses, you'll want to consider ways to further your reach, increase downloads and followers.

Consider researching podcasts that are either aligned or adjacent to yours. Reach out and see if they would be interested in cross-pollinating audiences for mutual gain.

There are podcasting magazines where you might find some of these and searching on iTunes is tried and true.

A ritual of keeping to your chosen format (weekly, monthly, etc.) makes promotion consistent.

# Chapter 11
# Monetization

It will take time and downloads before you are eligible for this. Expect to be upwards of 5-10,000 downloads before you can monetize with sponsors and advertisers. That download expectation is changing all the time.

Opportunity for advertising and sponsorship will generally be something you will offer in one of three places: beginning, midroll, or outro. Placement at the beginning is the most money. There is the possibility that your listeners will not listen until the end of the podcast, so because of that, the price for advertisers goes down if their placement is mid-roll or at the end.

Host-read advertising is always the best. If your listeners have come to respect you and your work, they will be more likely to buy what you share on the advertiser's behalf. It is part of the trust the host has built with their audience. Advertisers want to capitalize on that. A sponsor will be similar. But you are more likely to get an extended relationship with a sponsor who is more interested in the long game of your show. However, it does not mean that advertisers would not sign on for a month or three and extend it because they get the sale through your channel.

That having been said, there are times when you could realize something sooner. By bartering with another company that is interested in your podcast, maybe you can strike a balance. For example, they are selling skin products and to advertise on your podcast to your local following is interesting enough for them to offer a small commission for each set purchased.

Some hosting companies, like Podbean and Patreon, offer advertising assistance. As I'm writing this, I believe there is no charge to be considered for those advertising opportunities.

Affiliate Marketing with the likes of Amazon can be an option down the road so be sure to have your podcast registered on Audible which is their podcast platform.

If you see your podcast as a future community that you'd like to build events or conferences for, then monetization is a good idea to keep at the top of your mind. If you find your listeners are reaching out in large numbers, it might be an avenue to create a live or virtual event to test the waters.

Products like mugs, t-shirts, etc., can be used to build a following. Giveaways of your product to encourage sharing your podcast, etc.

Services can be tied into your content. If your podcast grows and you begin to offer consulting or other services, you can monetize here.

<u>Books</u> are a great way to move your content from audio into the hands of your following and potentially others who aren't aware of your podcast. You will become an expert on your subject and with each new guest, you'll learn more. This is an opportunity to publish articles, create eBooks, etc. The flipside of this, is that you will become a great guest for other podcasters who want to share your written work.

<u>Coaching and consulting</u> can be services you offer as well. In time, your voice will be one that your followers will want more from. You could offer 1:1 consulting with individuals and businesses.

<u>Speaking engagements</u> at a conference or live event could come from your coaching and/or consulting interactions.

<u>Memberships, Crowdfunding and Donations</u>:  You can reach out for support to your followers, listeners, friends and family. You can reach out to platforms like <u>Patreon</u>. This platform, for example, will be a place where you can play and offer things like bonus content.

<u>Premium Content</u>: This could be in the form of additional interviews, behind the scenes content, ad-free RSS feed, early access RSS feed, Q&A with the hosts or direct video access. This is definitely for later, but when you grow large enough, you can create a subscription model with a newsletter, videos, direct access to interviewees, etc.

<u>Newsletters</u> can be interesting because you capture the listeners email address and now you have direct access to

their eyes and ears. You are able to send outtakes, audiograms or answers to their questions. This could grow into a larger tool in the monetization piece for you. What I like about this is it also allows for deep dives on areas you were unable to explore due to the length of your podcast or the guest had to stop after 20 minutes. It's also a second avenue to capture advertising. Thus, creating another funnel of monetization.

# Chapter 12
# Finish Line

I'll end with this; we all have stories to tell. Your expertise, ideas, humor, whatever you bring to the table are worthy of a podcast.

In this guide, we have gone over everything from podcast art to podcast host to promoting your podcast.

Everything you need has been addressed. It is the definitive tool for launching an elegant and fully recognized podcast.

I'd like to extend a huge congratulations to you on successfully reaching this point. It means you are a podcaster now. It is worth celebrating.

*This huge achievement is all yours! I want to thank you for bringing me along on your journey.*

Send me a message on social media when you get here. Let me know what you built. Let's share your voice and the achievement of using Zero to Podcast to launch your podcast.

Happy Podcasting!

# AUTHOR BIO

This book is a culmination of the learning it took to create my podcast, <u>Culture Factor 2.0</u>. I wanted to be able to replicate that success over and over, so I wrote the book. Zero to Podcast is for you and for me!

My podcast, Culture Factor 2.0, is on all the platforms where you get your podcast fix. It recently won a Top Ten for Workplace and Company Culture podcasts. Additionally, I've had the tables turned and have been a Podcast Guest.

My background has been in corporate, hospitality, tradeshows and marketing. I think I'm best described as a Swiss-Army knife in marketing and business.

Next up? Building podcasts for businesses and individuals. I may even start a couple of other podcasts because I'm curious about many topics. And hopefully, getting others on their podcasting journey through my book, 'Zero to Podcast'.

## Find me on:

LinkedIn http://linkedin.com/in/hollyshannon1

Instagram @hollyeshannon

Twitter @HollyShannon_

Clubhouse at @hollyshannon

# AUTHOR'S NOTES & ACKNOWLEDGMENTS

Initially, I wrote this book for myself and by accident. I created this step-by-step guide because I knew that I would create more than one podcast. I don't like to reinvent the wheel. I did a ton of research, consulted people in the industry and broke things along the way and I took copious notes.

This was a labor of love to make it easy to create again and again. I now do this for companies and individuals.

Raz Cunningham is the Co-Founder of Little Fire and the producer of the Working Over Time podcast. We started around the same time in launching our podcasts. Never have I met a more generous person. He was giving of things he learned in the trenches and helped me as I transitioned to full creative rights of my podcast, Culture Factor 2.0. I'm not sure I would have made it through that if he wasn't so kind and non-judgmental of my mistakes and there were many. Note to reader; if you have made it this far, I cannot say it loud enough, "Have a Podcast PreNup if you are co-producing and/or co-hosting your podcast."

Nihal Salah, the Producer and Host of the podcast Content Marketing was instrumental in poking holes in my book. She made sure to point out what was missing and where I needed a deeper dive. I think the more intimate portraits within this book are because of her.

Maureen Edwards, whose expertise in photography upgraded my profile shots immediately. Her keen eye has also been pivotal in my podcast art, book cover and content. She's the most artistic person I trust with my image. Maureen is also a closet editor that wielded her red pen for this.

Christina Eanes, the Author of Life is an Escape Room and Secret to Super Productivity wrote a book that is also a successful podcast called Quit Bleeping Around. She was also there to answer a myriad of questions and continues to be an inspiration as she is launching something new every day!

Shira Atkins, the Founder of Wonder Media and Kinsey Grant of Morning Brew and the Host of Business Casual both gave me the inside perspective on how to interview and create a podcast. They were both generous with their time during a strange year in our collective history.

Nicole Damarjian is a budding podcaster. BirdieBound is coming soon as she took on the task of being my Beta Group. She has no experience in podcasting and admits to being technically challenged. This is why I chose her to use this step-by-step book to launch her podcast.

*And to you, the student, you have graduated!*

*You are a podcaster!*

*Share your voice and ideas!*

*Please share this book with anyone else looking to the brave, new world of podcasting!*

# BOOK DESCRIPTION

Want to start a podcast? This is where you begin.

- 12 chapter easy-to-follow guide
- Like the title, Zero to Podcast, it takes you from start to finish
- Make it a reality in a short time frame, with little or no money
- For the technically challenged or technically proficient
- Zero podcasting knowledge required

**Bottom line: when you finish this book, you will be a podcaster.**

# Your Personal Journal

*The rest of this book is your notebook, your journal. Think and write down everything about your podcast from topics to process. It'll be a great way to keep it all together in one place.*

Holly Shannon

_____

_____

_____

_____

_____

_____

_____

_____

_____

_____

_____

_____

_____

_____

_____

_____

_____

_____

_____

_____

_____

_____

_____

_____

_____

_____

_____

_____

_____

_____

_____

_____

_____

_____

_____

*This is for you. The creator in you. You may not see it yet, but by the end of this book, you will be calling yourself a podcaster.*

_____

_____

_____

_____

_____

_____

_____

_____

_____

_____

_____

_____

_____

_____

_____

_____

_____

_____

_____

_____

_____

_____

_____

_____

_____

_____

_____

_____

_____

_____

_____

_____

_____

_____

*Grow, be patient with yourself, think of your microphone as a hand weight. The more you lift it, the stronger you get.*

_____

_____

_____

_____

_____

_____

_____

_____

_____

_____

_____

_____

_____

_____

_____

_____

_____

_____

_____

1) *Ownership feels good.*

2) *Learning can be scary, but it makes you stronger.*

3) *If you don't know what you need, it is harder to ask for it and to ensure you get what you want.*

---
---
---
---
---
---
---
---
---
---
---
---
---
---

Holly Shannon

*You are so far along now! Keep going!*

Holly Shannon

*You must be close to launching that new podcast of yours.*

_____

_____

_____

_____

_____

_____

_____

_____

_____

_____

_____

_____

_____

_____

_____

*Congratulations!*

*Write down three things about your podcast that make you smile.*

*Share your podcast with the world and 'Zero to Podcast' if it was helpful!*

_____

_____

_____

_____

_____

_____

_____

_____

_____

_____

_____

_____

_____

_____

www.ingramcontent.com/pod-product-compliance
Lightning Source LLC
LaVergne TN
LVHW022125060326

832903LV00063B/4073